What the Pause Gives

poems by

Colleen Teasdale Filler

Finishing Line Press
Georgetown, Kentucky

What the Pause Gives

ACKNOWLEDGMENTS

I would like to dedicate this book to the students and teachers who fed me on
this journey with special thanks to Ellen Doré Watson and her writing groups
which led me to Drew University for my MFA and the community from Drew
that sustains my writing life.

Publisher: Leah Huete de Maines
Editor: Christen Kincaid
Cover Art: Path in the Woods, Vincent Van Gogh,
https://www.vangoghmuseum.nl/en/collection/s0080V1962
Author Photo: Kathryn Kimball
Cover Design: Elizabeth Maines McCleavy

Order online: www.finishinglinepress.com
also available on amazon.com

Author inquiries and mail orders:
Finishing Line Press
PO Box 1626
Georgetown, Kentucky 40324
USA

Contents

Backside of the Moon

Tadao Ando and James Turrel's Art House Project,
Naoshima, Japan

Twelve at a time, we enter the dark
inside the fire-cured cedar building,

hands trusting our palms along one wall,
around a corner, then along another,

walking slowly through the inky dark
like wading through a starless night sky

until my eyes no longer lead, no longer
reassure the body. Instead, we follow

orders, trust the touch, feel for the seat
where we are told to sit in complete blackness,

sit with the unknown, in silence, until
finally a faint light emerges on the far wall—

and a voice commands us to walk
towards a light that's hardly light, leave

our now safe darkness to move in the direction
of the gray, still not trusting our feet, unmoored

again, and I go slow in this shifted sense
of simple things like walking, sitting

in the immensity of otherness, untethered
from what I thought I knew.

Eben's Head

The trail winds toward a rocky shore
over webs of roots gnarled in their grasp—
through tufted hairgrass green in the forest,
gold in the openings, fighting for space
with wild raspberries near the shore—
clover, yarrow, orchard grass purple in the breeze.

Through the woods, the afternoon sun dapples
and brightens—a glow flows from moss—
soft lumps bulging over rolling rocks—
echoing the bulbous burls on scattered spruce—
abstract art with one, two, even three
separate round burstings in irregular places—
like water balloons swallowed and hardened—
and all around, trees in every stage of life
and death—green, gray, brown, and even
orange in the split from lightning strikes
the crack that comes from the weight of the wind—
upprooted trees with a mosaic of roots almost flat
and now vertical expose how feeble their grip
when spread over granite.

Eben's Head—blunt rocky bluff above the open
Atlantic—looking out to Brimstone,
then west to the Camden Hills, blue
and bumpy stretching across the horizon—water,
water, then the line of hills separating
vast stretches of ocean and sky.

August Morning on Isle au Haut

A hare paused in the road,
taking stock, ears alert—
dog in the woods
unaware behind me.

Twice I saw the pause—
then long leaps up the road—
hop, hop, leap
before disappearing into the woods.

Staying alert—
the key to staying alive.

Imprint Lurking

Whistler BC

Walking my dog
in the early morning,
suddenly he barks wildly.
Up the street, ambling across the road,
we see a large black bear
all too big, all too real.
We turn, walk the other way,
me wondering when
and where that bear will
emerge since it's headed
where we are heading.

Now every time I walk that way,
I see the bear.
It makes no sense. The bear is no longer
there yet it is always there.
Not a shadow but a big, black bear.
Something more powerful
than eyes. The eyes say
all clear. The mind says
beware.

Wind and Fire

The wind this morning in the Penobscot Bay—
ferocious—transports me from
love of its cleansing—
head leaning out the car window
or simply standing and feeling it blow
through me as I walk by the sea—

wind as power, as blessing
blowing the excess away,
that bones exposed-feeling—

wind as ominous
when it feeds flames—demons
set loose from long captivity—
suddenly free and consuming
anything in their path.

We are powerless against the licks
once they taste freedom.
Fire gallops through forests,
fields, homes reducing all
to orange, to embers in an instant.
Humbling. How little
we control our worlds.

What the Pause Gives

A cat peered out
from under a dark green yew
next to a red barn
set back from the road.

The cat gray and white.
Young. Big eyes.
Quiet. Watching.

A chance stopping
to adjust my bike seat.
In the pause,
I spotted the cat.

It took my stopping,
a shift in time.
I still think
about the cat,
about all the things

we don't see
when sights are set
and then when we stop,
what that pause brings.

The Arbutus Tree

Because I happened upon it one morning,

Because the lower bark flaked large reddish-brown slabs juxtaposed with smooth skin emerging from the rough,

Because the curve down low caught my eye, so unlike the many trees that rise straight up,

Because the color of the curve and the skin glowed—quinacridone gold-subtle Indian red-tarnished copper streaked with hints of violet,

Because the skin reminded me of the way my Art History professor described Ingres' painting of *La Grande Odalisque*—her shiny nude curves craving caress,

Because it felt brave and bare, irresistibly confident in its smoothness,

Because I couldn't walk by, couldn't resist rubbing the beautiful, brazen, bare limbs,

Because I am swept into a state, feeling the elation of the arbutus outside myself and inside at the same time, unable to contain, yet soaring.

Bone Broth

Two days of cooking on low—
lamb bones salvaged from luscious
meals—the pot stuffed with greens,
chopped ends of parsley,
carrot and onion peels
saved in the freezer—then add
the bay leaf and peppercorns,
two days for the good marrow—

the savory scent filled
the hemispheres of the house,
but two days of even low heat
saps so much. When I raised
the lid there was nothing
to find—nothing but
a burnished brine.

The goodness sucked out, gone.
Those wasted hours when
I simply forgot. Got distracted.
How easily we blind. How fortunate
that my house still stands.

Ladon Quartet

Cello, accordion, piano, percussion—not
your usual string quartet—and the cellist
flings her long hair aside so she can pluck
and bow with abandon—classical and klezmer—
while the Iranian pianist sometimes plucks inside the baby grand
like a harp when he's not playing poignant versions
of Chopin or sharing original compositions
inspired by flecks he sees in the morning light which the cellist
makes audible while the drummer sits wide legged on a wooden block
as he taps, brushes, and bangs it, then goes on to cymbals
and various other hand-held drums while the guy who is playing accordion
expands and contracts his face echoing its folds
as if they are his heart and lungs combined
and he sings from his soul as he taps his red and black patent saddle shoes
which send their own set of messages in case you had any doubt
how wild and free their music is and the when the boy
in the front row responds, his whole body bursting into dance,
his mom pulls him back, wraps him into his seat,
and I think of all the ways people might respond
to electric invitations and how instead we wrap ourselves
back into our chairs, clap, and jump to our feet
to thank the musicians for these hints of possibility.

Pomegranate

After Nazim Hikmet "On Living"

People whose faces I've never seen
may enjoy the same jokes,
feel the same wind.
We may wake to the same newscast,
gnawing burlap, flowing velvet.

Some of us plant olive trees
that take forty years to fruit,
and some dig in the trash
to find food for today.
If we find a pomegranate,
how great the joy.
Those that love the color
can say *I lived.*

The Little Beech Tree

Now in winter woods
widened with loss

bare everywhere,
easy to spot the beech—

the only leaves that
cling still, almost transparent

chiffon-like delicate
holding though battering

by wind, by glacial weather—
hold out, hold on,

and the trunk's skinny adolescence,
extraordinary long arms reach out

unusual in a forest where
all goes up and up.

We trample a carpet of other
leaves, brown and long gone.

I try to imprint the spot,
locate neighbors, hillside,

so when the forest warms and
fills full and green,

I can find this polished
gray doing its dance—

a slender David
surrounded by goliaths.

Tornado in Western Massachusetts

February 26, 2017

A split second shift brought wind howling
through trees, turning the sky yellow/green,
placid air seized with fury, temper unfurled,
doors blown open, wind unleashed
upon our town with leap-frogged slashing.

The next day, the sun shone innocently
through the same air, sky benevolent blue,
snow littered with pine needles
and splinters—branches and whole trees

thrashed, smashed, as if toothpicks.
Giant trees downed, parts of houses
simply gone, a large barn destroyed
next to an untouched house—

a kitchen in the front of one house
gone, exposing the back rooms
like a doll house—

Mid-May

Some acorns crack open in spring—
glow lime, yellow, raspberry pink,
tendrils tender as tongues, inner
organs—esophagus, lungs, uterus.

Tentative, they reach out, seek
ground. Some latch in, begin
to grow. Maybe they become
a twig, launch a leaf or two.

And all around, so many still
stay brown, round underfoot.
So few trees amidst
so many possibilities.

Roots

Crusted with bark, pace slowed to ponder,
I study how trees meet the ground.
Some shoot straight down, seamless stakes
driven into soil—telephone pole perpendicular—
but others have more visible grip—
toes bulge, buttress the base,
gnarled feet stretch over ledge
or extend like octopus arms, reaching
in multiple directions, petticoats of full
skirts with lace-like webs revealing
what is often hidden underground.

What's underneath matters. Slabs of rock
won't let roots in. They must crawl across
granite, seek a path, vulnerable pink, yellow,
green tenders staking out a journey.

And then there are the nursing trees—
new ones fed from the decay of the old,
fresh rising through what looks like picket
fences—the mark of ancient cedars or
roots arched above ground where
the ground below has washed away—
tree still rooted enough to stand.

Savoring Summer

We are in the lake. It doesn't have
a color. Our heads appear unattached
to bodies. Trees crowd the shore,
maples shimmering silver in the wind,

while cedar trunks roll down the rocks
before they rise—like elephant trunks
thick and wrinkled extending down
toward the water then up, up, reaching

supple yet strong, flowing yet firm,
majestic as Mayan sculptures,
monumental in shape and size,
curves contrasting with straight maples

while above, crystalline blue lucidity,
made more blue by piled puffs
of white, fresh snow-white, with
blue that goes singing as it lifts

us from the lake
even as we stay, weightless—

Standing Guard

Lining the field—jagged gray,
riddled with holes,

wind wracked,
silent, broken limbs,

thick peeling shards of bark
speak years of weathering,

all that time shading cows,
sharing sap for syrup,

shadows of their former
selves, they still stand

majestic maples,
elegant in their aging.

Water

Beet stains drip from colander
to counter—hearts so red
that must be cut—thumbs
and fingers stained by beet touch,
so much water for the hands,
faucet running, water flowing
caution floating, I'm adrift
seeing women carrying water
poles with buckets, vase on head,
searching water, crying children
tears propel a frantic search—
there no faucets, dream of faucets
people walk for miles and miles
mirage of faucets, mirage of water

and all the while I watch it flow
out of faucet, spilling water
scatter stain of beets so sweet
watch the waste with sense of wonder
clean the counter, clean the hand
keep the vision, vase on heads
walking over too dry land.

Dreaming Apricots

I'm perched in my grandfather's apricot tree
surrounded by plump globes of pale orange
slightly fuzzy, just right ripe fruit
lit like lights on a Christmas tree.

Everywhere apricots
and even when I eat more than my fill,
I still haven't made a dent.
in the plentitude surroundings me,

because it was cared for and thrives
in the dry sunny ground of OK Falls, BC,
gloriously feeding me on this perfect day,
ten years old and no one to call me down.

Tsunami Signals

Animals know. They pick up slow
rumblings, hear the prelude,
know in their bones something
sonar, something bending
that soon will break—

the rubbing of plates against each other—
unstable porcelain that though fired
will not withstand the thrust
the earth will throw—

unleashing venom in the water,
helpless in the hands
of such power, forces
let go—forces animals feel

in their body wisdom—
they know what will come.
They have no words—
knowledge locked in their bodies

they tremble
then they run.

Skunk Cabbage

The skunk cabbage is not one thing.
The roots hide and hold themselves under
all winter. Little green spikes emerge
early in spring, when snow melts
in the swampy bogs where they thrive.

Slowly the spikes are joined by frills,
leafy lime punctuation in the wet brown
surrounds and the frills keep creeping
up as if testing the air. Once they look
well established, a knob like spike appears—

yellow spadix, textured like corn cob,
sheathed in florescent yellow spathe,
screaming to be noticed,
some version of a mating dance,
some version of flashy fashion

that repeats itself year after year,
variety coming from the season not
the demand for new, new,
each year until a repeat
slips in again (short skirts,

pleated pants, wide legs). The phallic
corn surrounded by larger
bright green leaves until they manifest
at least three feet tall, enormous tropical
blooming, and still the bears

have not come. Clearly they have found
food elsewhere, but I'm told they too
like clockwork come, foraging, finishing,
and then what's left will die out until
the snow, then disappear again.

I wonder how much we are like this plant—
poking our heads out, supported by so much
ground until we don the frills, drop the sheath,
see what we do in the open air, enjoy
our season, then find ourselves underground.

Do we feel some essential connection?
know we too have a cycle? what you see
will not stay From afar, predictable.
But how much we try to say
Look at me, I'm different.

Still Life

On a crate, a cup, a shadow
half eaten by the murky light
murky cup half gone for days
now no chance of halo leaking
light, shadow like the faintest
curtain, shades of grey instead
of white, shadow like a layer
over specimen not seeping life
shadow shows no sign of halo
grey and dark of almost night

murk upon half eaten mattress
no holy halo holy light
murk upon the crate, the cup,
murk that filters day from night

something pinned upon the mattress
sloughed by day and sloughed by night,
cup upon the crate still lurking
stench has leaked beyond the glass,
shadows leering, shadows lurking
night about to close its clasp.

Whistler Bells

There's a stillness in the bells—
tucked silent in the woods facing Alta Lake,
thick, strong beams forming the frame
for their perpendicularity.

They hang facing the water and the northern
Garibaldi Range—one long cylinder surrounded
by a squat square and a three dimensional
triangle, three clappers like singular cable earrings

hanging from their metal bellies—
contrasting with the supple curves of trees
and bushes, the long expanse of lake. Suspended
in air, these man-made geometries

invite hands to ignite the strike,
set metal on metal clanging side to side,
the touch that sends three distinct waves
vibrating from inner ear to outer air,

alerting eyes to awaken and sharpen,
to see and feel this lake, these snow-capped mountains,
this sky, skin to air, feet on soggy ground,
the purity of sound unbound.

Grim Reflection

Fate succumbs many a species: one alone jeopardises itself.
Auden, "Marginalia"

It used to be that hitting
the high-water mark
was aberrant—the storm
of the century

but now, it's a portent
of things to come—
a feeling of gloom,
because we know

what we suck from the earth—
fracking oil, mining neodymium,
driving cars, flying in planes
that suck gas,

In our hearts, we know
and still,
we cannot help ourselves.

We travel thousands of miles
 to conference about the state
of the earth, consuming, consuming.
We know it continues the cycle,

but still we can't stop taking—
greed over grief. We cannot
help ourselves.

Animal Behavior

We are on the homestretch coming down the hill when Ricky
emerges in front of me, rabbit dangling from his mouth. My
shocked *Drop it* worked to reveal a sweet bundle of flecked gray
and brown fur, startled eyes. It lay for a moment still on the
ground, then hopped with front legs, dragging the back ones
behind. I don't have to say sickening. I didn't cry. It was deeper
than cry. He was being a dog but even he didn't seem to know
what to do. Maybe his first catch after numerous hunts. He
watched the bunny drag himself off, disappearing into the high
grass. Conflicted, part wanting an ambulance, prioritizing getting
the dog away, we fled. Next day, Rick sniffed and looked, circling
the area where we had last seen the bunny. It was not to be found.
Hard to know if it lived. No evidence either way.

Song of the Wolves

Paul Winter howls the wolf's wail
through his saxophone

transporting a Massachusetts auditorium
to a cold Minnesota night

where wolves fill the dark sky
and lurk the land. The saxophone sings

songs of fur and teeth distilled
in the shiny horn.

Imagine silver fur running freely
over snow, owning sky.

The saxophone song—
all beauty, no terror now—

invites us to feel
the Minnesota night

and let loose that howl
we rarely sing.

What Endures

Travel-weary, drenched by rain,
we lighted upon Vezelay
just as pilgrims for centuries
drawn to the relics of Mary Magdalene

we were lured by the familiar name
in an unfamiliar countryside—rural
and wet—the promise of the church
atop the hill, the respite, the carvings—

and yet, the rain gushed down the gutters,
a night to be home—not far from home,
not witness to stones smooth from years
of copious flow, flowing torrentially down.

Inside the church, the music of Hildegarde
von Bingen resonated resilience—she who when women
were bound to men, found a way to unleash
herself, to signal strengths unleashing still—

she with a legacy of botany, medicine, philosophy,
chants sacred even now—a thousand years
later, and in this rainy town on this gloomy night,
a small, white robed woman walked from the dark

of this thousand-year-old church into a transept of light
filling the church with thousand-year-old sound, Hildegard
enduring through the centuries, transporting me beyond self,
spirited by this gift to women, to all who soar with her.

Fat and Feathers

In summer, a purple smoke bush sheltered a nest
where we watched the bright blue eggs
and near-embryos,
seeing hearts pump and blood flow
through translucent skin.

At first, feathers were barely fuzz.
Ten days, we watched
anxious beaks hoist upwards
as fat and feathers accumulated
on their bodies. One of the four eggs
disappeared, and though we had seen
a beak and fuzz, it didn't linger.
Another stayed, glowing in opalescence
long after the healthy two departed.

By fall, my mother lay in her hospital bed,
bones visible through disappearing skin,
not luminescent but certainly bird-like,
beak open, awaiting food from her babes,
heart pumping, thirsting for life.
Many times, I thought through goodbyes,
but she kept resurrecting herself.

We are but skin and fuzz,
varying degrees of will and muscle,
never knowing when the fat,
when the feathers.

In The Dream

I was—and perhaps we—
were sorting in a barn—
who knows whose barn?
whose stuff?

and I gathered some gifts
for my mom but
when I went to present
them, I only had one—

a peach-colored nightgown
and she was cold and
I was speechless and
it doesn't matter

that she is seven
years dead—somehow
that need to please,
that sense of lost love

no reaching can reach,
something empty sits and sits,
something that is not
comforted by death.

Running "The Dish" at Stanford

My rhapsody came from defying
gravity, finding the elements

that transcend the body, seeking
steel for structure, step by step,

day after day striding the miles
through those hills, their yellowed folds

rolling and rising. I savored
those oaks, big and gnarled,

more bark than leaf,
knowing time,

so that even years of drought
did not destroy their domination.

They stand and rule,
inviting worship, these icons,

blessings without church
or pew or sermon.

They gnarl me still
as they rise in my mind

enduring all weather,
all seasons, rising.

Hardwired

My sheep dog barks wildly
at what he perceives
as danger—gulls squawking
searching for fish, crows cackling,
a huge wing-spanned heron.
He's been programmed
over hundreds of years
to be on the lookout for birds—
to give warning, save the baby
lambs. We can't seem to de-program
this burning need. It's a hardwire—

and I wonder what hardwiring
sets me off—if my survival
is such that I learn
to ignore atrocities
if they're far enough away,
if it's someone else,
if I feel helpless—
killing off parts of myself.

Winter Woods

Walking in the near dark
well bundled, I feel the teeth
of winter sharpening.

Warning—skin prickles,
hair on end, feeling
bare to the bones.

How close we are
to the edge. A night
of this could kill.

The Reckoning

It's Christmas in Hyde Park and from
the far reaches of the world, people

flock—Arab and Asian, hijabs, hats, flowing
fabric from bundled bodies facing the chill

of British winter and throngs line up to see
the changing of the guard, red coats, bearskin

hats—crowds bowing to ritual that regulates
what might well be rowdy—results of years

when tea and spice flowed out of Sri Lanka
and Singapore, when excess Englishmen

went off to rule continents, carve boundaries,
rake in the riches that kept the British Isles afloat,

kept the royals looking regal. Now the country
teems with their former subjects, the sea

no longer much of a moat. It's Christmas
in London and the empire has come home to roost.

Reasons to Survive

Man carrying a curly headed three-year-old.
Must be the father, I think.

Who says love is abstract? It's there
in the hold—invisible made visible

by the gentle grip under the butt,
the inclination towards,

the dance in the eyes,
the spring in the step,

energy field extending through and around
saying how good to hold you, you are not

weight but light, you give me reason
to be, and the man meets my gaze

and smiles without force and says hello
and bids the boy to do the same

teaching that embracing the world
means more embracing, compounding

interest and a little sun shines on this not
so sunny day and as they pass, lightness

in the man's step, his oh so happy to hold you
step, the little owl backpack on the big man's

back, the little big-eyed owl who will stay
awake with that child, watching him,

carrying his familiar things when
his loving father parts, connecting him

to the love that he came from like a seed
growing in the spring of this hungry world.

Colleen Teasdale Filler has been writing in her head and on scraps of paper for as long as she can remember. When she was teaching seventh and ninth grade English, she started to take her poetry more seriously, and in retirement, she earned an MFA in Poetry from Drew University. She has been published in several journals including the *Lupine Review, The Island Reader,* and *Stanford Magazine,* but mostly, she writes for herself and participates in several writing groups connected to her long-term Massachusetts home and her teachers and colleagues from Drew. Thanks to Zoom, these relationships are alive and well, even with her current eight-month residency in British Columbia and her summer months in Maine. She is blessed with a long-term marriage, three adult children, and four grandchildren. She practices Iyengar yoga and teaches community yoga while in Maine. She loves to spend time with her grandchildren, walk her dog Ricky, read, swim anywhere, ski, and paint with watercolors.

.